Step by Step
FOLK ART FLOWERS

Step by Step
FOLK ART FLOWERS

EVA TUMMEL

Kangaroo Press

I dedicate this book
to all my students
with whom I have spent many happy
hours of painting

Reprinted in 1995
First published in 1994 by Kangaroo Press Pty Ltd
3 Whitehall Road Kenthurst NSW 2156 Australia
P.O. Box 6125 Dural Delivery Centre NSW 2158
Printed in Hong Kong through Colorcraft Ltd

ISBN 0 86417 558 2

CONTENTS

Introduction   7
What is Bauernmalerei?   8
Motifs   8
Materials   10
Round Brush Technique   10
Brushes   11
Materials for Beginners   11
Base-Coating   12
Marbling   12
Sponging   12
Project Preparation: Wood   13
Painting on Tin   13
Project Preparation: Terracotta   14
Leaves   15
Daisies   19
  Large designs   20
  Small designs   26
  Borders   30

Roses   35
  Designs   38
  Borders   43
  Rosebuds   44
Tulips   49
  Designs   52
  Borders   53
Hearts   59
  Designs   60
  Borders   61
Birds   67
  Designs   68
Wildflowers   77
  Designs   78
  Borders   82
Lettering   85
Index   88

Floral alphabet (see page 85)

INTRODUCTION

Dear Folks

In my previous books, *Folk Art with Australian Flowers* and *Folk Art on Terracotta*, I have given you examples of finished painted articles, on the centre pages illustrating the leaves step by step. I have had an overwhelming number of people writing to me saying how easy they found it to follow the instructions and could I please illustrate more flowers, so that they could learn to paint them step by step.

Folk Art Flowers Step by Step is my response to these requests. I bring you a large number of leaves and flowers step by step, designs that will demonstrate to you how to use different flowers and make up your own designs, and also how to design your own borders.

The old *Bauernmalerei* ('farmers' painting') is mostly painted with strong colours—reds, yellows, blues, greens and black. Being of European origin I am influenced by this and favour the simple designs and clear colours mostly found in Bavarian and Hungarian designs.

My introduction to folk art came at an early age. I was born in Hungary of Austrian and Hungarian parents and spent most of my school holidays at my grandparents' place. I spent many happy hours sketching and painting in the garden or the vegie patch, painting my grandmother's terracotta milk jugs. The only problem was that I was only allowed to use watercolours, therefore every day when the jugs were washed there went my designs—so I painted them again! Doing this certainly gave me a lot of good practice in comma strokes.

As a teenager I came to Australia. I studied Advertising and Commercial Art in Melbourne and for thirty years worked as a greeting card designer with a number of publishers.

My many years of experience as an artist have been very beneficial to my creation of my own designs and colour schemes for folk art patterns. I have been painting folk art since the early sixties, a time when this art was not widely known in Australia.

I have taught folk art in Victoria and South Australia and for the past eight years have been teaching in Queensland. My daughter Nicole and I opened 'Folklore House', the first Folk Art Studio in Queensland, six years ago, from where we still teach privately. We also teach larger groups of people through Adult Education in a number of TAFE colleges—two in Brisbane and two on the Sunshine Coast.

Two years ago I also started my own Folk Art Club at the request of many country people who live in isolation and can't get to any classes or shops. Through our Club we help them with as much information as possible. If you are interested in joining our Club write to Eva Tummel's 'Country Folk Art Club', PO Box 646 Nambour Queensland 4560.

I hope you get many hours of pleasure painting the flowers and designs from this book.

Happy Painting!

WHAT IS BAUERNMALEREI?

Bauernmalerei or Farmers' Painting, Folk Art or Cottage Art, is definitely an art and not a craft! Bauernmalerei is a very simple but effective form of art that dates back to the sixteenth or seventeenth century. We find some beautiful pieces in museums throughout Europe.

Motifs originally had strong symbolic meanings, mostly religious. The designs were always simple and mostly floral, scenic, animal or religious scenes. Styles were different in Bavaria, Austria and Switzerland, and it was possible to determine the origin of a painting from the way the flowers were painted.

Bauernmalerei was practised mostly by farmers. During long winter months they would make simple furniture and decorate it with paint work. Beautiful inlaid furniture was in fashion, which only the very rich could afford, so the peasants made their own pieces and painted them with intricate and colourful designs.

German artists have identified that Bauernmalerei developed from the influence of four major artistic periods: the Renaissance, the Baroque, the Rococo and the Biedermeier.

Renaissance (sixteenth to seventeenth centuries)
The work was done on untreated wood and the patterns of the inlaid wood were imitated with stencils. Designs were symmetrical; the motifs used were mostly six-pointed stars, double-headed eagles and checked patterns. Colours were limited to black, or black and red.

Baroque (first half of the eighteenth century)
The wood was completely covered with paint. The surfaces were divided into panels. The symmetrical designs of the Renaissance became more colourful, richer and lively.

Rococo (second half of the eighteenth century)
The symmetry was looser. The colours were mainly light and delicate. Flowers looked more natural. Shells and scrolls were simplified with flowers worked through them.

Biedermeier (first half of the nineteenth century)
The influence of Biedermeier was unmistakeable. Bouquets of flowers were more modest and often bound together with a bow. The interest of the surface was increased primarily with timber grain imitation.

Today's Bauernmalerei is the combination of the traditional and one's own ideas. Bauernmalerei is not pure copying but a creative occupation combining both old and new. The basis for progression is always the traditional Bauernmalerei, however, for it teaches us various painting techniques, styles and colours.

There is a renewed interest today in Bauernmalerei, possibly a reaction to the uniformity of mass produced articles. By painting one's own designs and using one's own colour scheme, items become more personalised.

MOTIFS

In Bauernmalerei flowers and motifs always had symbolic meanings, mostly religious.

Flowers were always placed in containers, urns or pots, symbolising the water of life. Today we mostly use baskets or bows to tie together the flowers. The flowers most commonly used are roses, tulips, daisies, carnations and lilies.

Another very important motif in Bauernmalerei is the Tree of Life, with different flowers painted from the same stem. This symbolises eternal renewal, growth and vitality.

The fruits most frequently used are grapes, pomegranates, apples, pears and berries of all kinds.

Animals are often used, not on their own but as part of a design, the most commonly used being birds, fish, deer, two-headed eagles, horses, cows, ducks and roosters.

Heart—symbol of Love

Tulip—flame in Christ

Rose—symbol of Christ

Pomegranate—symbol of Christ

Grapes—blood of Christ

Sun—symbol of Life

*Carnation—symbol of
hands and nails of Christ*

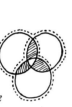

*Rings—sign for the
Holy Trinity*

Tree of Life

*Cross—symbol of light
and holiness*

Protection against evil

Symbol of prosperity

*Protection against
evil spirits*

*Fish—symbol of Life
and Fertility*

Sign for Earth

Urn—water of Life

MATERIALS

Paints

Waterbased acrylic paints (artist's colours). Make sure they are good quality. There are at least five different brands of paints presently on the market, and some are better quality than others. I leave the choice to you but please experiment with all of them to decide which brand you prefer to use.

There are at least fifty to a hundred different colours available in most brands. You will find, however, that if you purchase the primary colours plus a few other colours, you will be able to mix at least another fifty shades or more. Decorative colours come in 50 ml bottles or 75 ml tubes. Base coat colours come in 250 ml bottles or jars.

Varnishes

Waterbased polyurethane varnish (non-yellowing) is available in satin or gloss finish in 250 ml bottles. Use a soft fibre flat brush 12 mm or 25 mm (½'' or 1'') wide. Apply varnish with even strokes in *one* direction only. Try not to go over the same strokes again. On most articles two coats of varnish are sufficient, but you may apply three or four coats for extra gloss and durability.

I have found from my own experience in the past that different batches of varnishes can vary a lot. I suggest you try them out first on a trial piece (something small), before you take the plunge to varnish your project. Do read the instructions given by the manufacturers on bottles carefully.

I normally leave my work for 24 hours before I apply the first coat of varnish. Leave overnight to dry and then apply the second coat. Sand gently between coats. Avoid varnishing in a draught or in front of a fan. Also try to avoid very humid and rainy days, as varnish tends to bubble in these conditions.

Most varnishes have a slightly milky appearance when applied, but should dry to a clear finish. Please make sure you use a soft good-quality brush for varnishing, otherwise the brush will create streakiness.

All Purpose Sealer

This is a very important medium that should be used in all base coat colours.

Some base coat paints already have sealer in them, so make sure you check for this on the instruction label. Sealer also plays an important part in bonding the paint to any surface you are preparing to paint.

Flow Medium

Flow medium makes the paint much easier to handle, because when it is added to paint it makes it flow nicely. Some brands already have flow medium in them, so check label before use. Mix one part of flow medium to one part paint. This medium is very good to use in hot weather, or when you are painting curlicues. It is also helpful when doing lettering. You will find when doing fine long strokes that when flow medium is added your brush will not run out halfway through the stroke.

Crackling

When using crackle medium you must work fast, as crackle medium won't work after 24 hours. This means you must finish the project in one day.

1. After cleaning article, paint with one coat of base coat colour mixed with sealer and let dry. Next, apply in rapid succession four coats of base coat colour, this time paint only. Let dry in between coats.
2. Trace design onto article and paint. Designs should be kept simple so you can paint them on in a short time.
3. As soon as design is dry, apply thick coat of crackle medium all over article.
4. Place in a warm area (under a desk light is ideal). Within 20 minutes small cracks will appear. Do not use a hairdryer.

Retarder and Antiquing Medium

This is good to use in warm dry conditions, because it prolongs the drying time of paints. When using this medium allow your project to dry for a longer period than usual before varnishing. After you have painted the piece apply one coat of varnish and let it dry. To antique your work choose a colour you would like to use. Mix 1 part paint to 1 part retarder and antiquing medium. Brush this mixture gently onto your painted piece. Wipe back with a paper towel. If you wipe back straight away you will achieve a light antiquing. If you leave the mixture on for a longer period of time you will achieve a darker effect. I find this method is only good to use on older pieces of furniture, as it gives you that really old-looking finish.

ROUND BRUSH TECHNIQUE

Comma Stroke

Commas are the most important and easiest strokes in folk art painting. They can look very effective amongst different designs and as fill-in strokes.

When loading your brush for commas make sure you load the brush so that a rounded head is obtained when you begin to paint the stroke.

Press down gently on your surface to begin. Then start gradually pulling the brush towards you, releasing the pressure on the brush half-way through the stroke.

Make sure you come to a complete stop before lifting your brush off the surface. Do not flick the brush at the end of the stroke, as you will end up with a so-called 'fish tail'. This is a result of losing control of the brush.

The S Stroke
Start with the tip of the brush, and begin to pull it towards you, adding some pressure. Then continue adding more pressure as your stroke begins to go the other way, then gradually release the pressure.

Finish your stroke by bringing the brush to a point, stop and then lift the brush from your work. The most pressure should be applied in the middle part of the stroke.

Scrolls and Curlicues
With this stroke you can have a lot of fun. You can make the scrolls curly, or make all sorts of patterns with them. A scroll can be either thick or thin—it depends on what sort of pressure you apply. You can achieve this stroke best with a liner brush, but you can also use a #00 round.

C Stroke
To start this stroke you must begin with the top of the C. The brush *must* be perpendicular to the painting surface. Start pulling gently, then start to apply pressure gradually as you are entering the curved part of the stroke.

This is the thickest part of the stroke. When leaving the centre of the curve start gently releasing pressure, and finish your stroke with a fine line. Come to a complete stop and lift brush off surface.

BRUSHES

I recommend good quality synthetic fibre or synthetic sable brushes. Pure sable brushes are not suitable for folk art painting nor for use with acrylic paints.

I only use round brushes for painting my designs, as the old traditional folk art was always done with round brushes. With round brushes you achieve a much softer effect. The only time I use flat brushes is for base coating or varnishing.

The round brushes I use most are sizes #00, #2, #4, #6 and #8. I use a liner brush (#1) to paint finer detail work such as stems and curlicues. A flat brush 25 mm (1'') wide or a #12 round brush is recommended for base-coating, and for varnishing

use a flat brush 25 mm (1'') wide—it must be soft fibre.

Brush Care
If quality brushes are taken care of properly they will last for many years. Some of my brushes are over 30 years old and are still in perfect condition because of the way I have looked after them.

Loading of Brushes
When you are loading a brush never let the paint reach the ferrule (metal part), as the paint will build up inside the ferrule, dry, and split the fibres. This means you lose the point on your brush. The paint should only be loaded to halfway (at the most three-quarters) up the fibre of the brush.

Rinse frequently between strokes. When you have finished painting make sure to rinse the brush thoroughly so that there is no paint left in the fibres.

A handy hint I always give my students is to roll the brush once you have cleaned it onto a cake of soap. Shape the brush to a point, then just stand it upright in either a brush holder or glass jar. This will keep your brushes in shape. The soap will dry but will not ruin your brush—you can leave it in for any length of time. Before using again rinse the brush out in cold water.

MATERIALS FOR BEGINNERS

Paints
At least 8 to 10 colours in waterbased acrylic paints (specially designed for folk art painting).

Brushes
4 basic brushes (good quality synthetic fibre)—
#00, #2, #4, #6 round for painting designs.
1 flat brush 25 mm (1'') width, or #12 round brush.
1 flat brush 25 mm (1'') width for varnishing, must be soft fibre.

Varnish
1 bottle of polyurethane waterbased varnish (not household varnish). Satin or gloss finish.

All Purpose Sealer
1 bottle.

Palette
Round palette (10 small dishes, 1 large in centre).

Wooden Articles
Pine or plywood or craft wood.
For information on wooden articles and Country Folk

Art Club membership write to Mrs Eva Tummel, 'Folklore House', PO Box 646 Nambour Queensland 4560.

Pencils

2B for drawing designs and tracing patterns.
5H for transferring design onto project.
White, black or peach colour carbon pencils for freehand drawing.

Tracing Paper, Rubber and Transfer Paper

Black, white or yellow.

Sketch Pad

For practice strokes and colour combinations, also for creating your own designs.

Sandpaper

Wet-and-dry #400 or #600.

And

Water jar to rinse your brushes in. Spray mist bottle to moisten the paint occasionally and prevent it from drying up. Freezer bag to cover palette, preserving paint in between uses. Paints in palette will last for weeks if you look after them.

Finishes

Every project completed must have a good finish—without that your work is incomplete. Paint every surface of a project—front, back, sides and insides. Varnish all your projects—it will protect them from dust and dirt, and highlight the colours used for painting.

To store leftover or excess paint, use small airtight jars or plastic film canisters. Leftover paint also can be used for base-coating smaller articles—wooden spoons, small boxes, fridge magnets—or painting the insides of small boxes.

N.B. No responsibility is taken by the artist or the publishers of this book for any articles spoiled due to using inferior materials, or not taking proper care!

BASE-COATING

Base-coating is a very important part of preparing your project, and of achieving a well finished article. You have two main choices with base coat paints:
1. Base coat paint with no added all purpose sealer.
   In this case you must mix 1 part paint to 1 part all purpose sealer. Paint first coat with sealer mixture, second coat apply paint only.

2. Base coat paint with all purpose sealer already added. In this case just apply two coats of paint. Make sure you sand between coats.

A third option you might like to experiment with is as follows: First apply straight all purpose sealer on your project. Then apply a coat of 1:1 all purpose sealer plus paint. Follow this with 1 coat of paint only.

Remember that whichever procedure you use it is a must to sand between each coat to get a nice smooth finish. With most base coat colours 2 coats are sufficient; however, with lighter or transparent colours in certain brands, you may need 3 or 4 coats to achieve a good coverage.

In most brands of waterbased acrylic artist's colours formulated especially for folk art painting you will find a large range of base colours which come in 250 ml bottles or jars. Use these for base-coating, as they are more economical. Use the tube paints, which are more expensive, for leaves and flowers only. Please do not use ordinary household paints for base coating, as most are toxic and they do not give the same finish. It is also dangerous to mix household paints with other paints because a chemical reaction can occur. For example, the design can peel off or come off while you are varnishing. Most of all, though, it can be extremely dangerous for people who suffer from certain allergies.

MARBLING

To achieve this effect you apply 2 contrasting layers of paint. When you are applying the second layer, use a wider brush and gently swirl at random through the colours.

Next take a feather and, using the tip, drag it through the paint to achieve a marbled effect. Marbling is mostly used on larger pieces, for example, on the sides of a cabinet or wardrobe. You never paint a design over the areas which you have marbled.

SPONGING

This gives a nice effect, especially when used on terracotta. As for marbling you apply 2 contrasting layers of paint. Allow the first colour to dry completely before applying the second colour. While it is still wet, dab over the surface with a sponge. It's as easy as that.

PROJECT PREPARATION: WOOD

Proper preparation before painting an article is very important in achieving a well finished product. Here are a few suggestions for the most common surfaces.

New Wood
Painted solid background colour.
1. Fill in cracks and holes with wood putty, let dry.
2. Sand with #400 wet-and-dry sandpaper.
3. Apply 1 coat of base coat colour with 12 mm (½'') flat brush.
   First coat: mix 1 part paint and 1 part sealer.
4. Let dry. Sand lightly, wipe off any dust with a lint-free cloth.
5. Apply second coat of base colour, let dry.
   Second coat: paint only!
6. Project is now ready to apply design and paint.

Old Wood
Painted solid background colour.
1. Remove dust and dirt, grease marks and old polish. Clean surface with soapy water or sugar soap.
2. Fill in cracks and holes with wood putty, let dry.
3. Sand with #400 wet-and-dry sandpaper.
4. Apply 1 coat of base coat colour with 12 mm (½'') flat brush.
   First coat: mix 1 part paint and 1 part sealer.
5. Let dry. Sand lightly, wipe off any dust with a lint-free cloth.
6. Apply second coat of base coat colour. Let dry.
   Second coat paint only.
7. Project is now ready to apply design and paint.

Natural Wood
If you prefer to leave the timber a natural colour you must first seal it with 1 coat of all purpose sealer, let it dry, then sand lightly and proceed with painting.

Pre-painted Wood
If a wooden article has been painted before, there is no need to strip back the paint completely—just clean and sand well. Proceed with the same method of preparation as above.

Add sealer to first coat, but second coat paint only. Project is now ready to apply design and paint.

Finish
Allow project to dry (let the paint cure) for at least 24 hours before applying varnish. Apply 1 coat of varnish. Let dry. Sand gently with #400 wet-and-dry sandpaper, then apply second coat of varnish.

You have the choice of either satin or gloss polyurethane waterbased varnish.

STAINING TECHNIQUE FOR WOOD

Staining can look very effective, especially when you are working with an attractive piece of natural pine. It really brings the grain out. For staining you may use any colour you wish; just follow this procedure:
1. Dampen the wooden article all over with a sponge. This is to prevent the stain soaking in too quickly, which creates a blotchy or uneven effect.
2. Apply stain to one side first with a sponge or base coat brush. Wipe off excess paint with paper towel. Let dry.
3. Apply stain to sides and back of the article. Let dry. Before applying the design to a wooden article sand gently with #400 sandpaper.

MIXING STAIN

1 part paint
1 part all purpose sealer
1 part retarder
. . . part water

Depending on how deep a colour you wish the stain to be, you can add more or less water. Repeat the staining procedure until you achieve the shade you want.

PAINTING ON TIN

New Tin
1. Clean well, sand lightly.
2. Paint with primer or spray with rust proof solution. Let dry. The project is now ready for base-coating.

Old Tin
1. Clean well (you can use oven cleaner).
2. Remove rust by sanding or sandblasting.
3. Paint with primer or spray with rust proof solution. It is very important to remove all rust, as all waterbased acrylic paints will let rust through in time.

The project is now ready for base-coating.

PROJECT PREPARATION: TERRACOTTA

Proper preparation before painting a project is very important in achieving a well finished product. Use these techniques for preparing and base-coating terracotta:

Terracotta (natural)
1. Clean terracotta article thoroughly. If you use a damp cloth to remove dust and dirt, make sure you dry the article well before proceeding with painting.
2. Sand lightly with wet-and-dry sandpaper, wiping off any dust with lint-free cloth.
3. Trace design from book onto tracing paper with 2B pencil.
4. Position design on terracotta item, placing white or black transfer paper between tracing paper and project.
5. Retrace design with 5H pencil. You might have to cut the pattern in half and trace one half first, then the other, as most terracotta items are rounded, making it hard to transfer designs. Try to freehand some of the designs.
6. Project is now ready to paint. Follow painting guide for each project.

Note:
1. You can paint straight onto terracotta.
2. You can paint terracotta with one coat of all purpose sealer before painting.
3. You can add a few drops of sealer to each colour.

Terracotta (coloured background)
First base coat: 1 part paint + 1 part all purpose sealer.
Second base coat: Paint only.
1. Clean terracotta article thoroughly. If you use a damp cloth to remove dust and dirt, make sure you dry the article well before proceeding with base coat colour.
2. Sand lightly with wet-and-dry sandpaper, wipe off any dust with lint-free cloth.
3. Apply first coat of base coat colour mixed with all purpose sealer using 12 mm (½'') flat brush or #12 round brush. Let dry well before applying second coat of colour.
4. Paint second coat of base coat colour, this time paint only. (If a third coat is necessary for better coverage apply paint only.)
5. Trace design from book onto tracing paper with 2B pencil.
6. Position design on terracotta item, placing white or black transfer paper between tracing paper and project.
7. Retrace design with 5H pencil. Try to freehand some of the design.
8. Project is now ready to paint. Follow painting guide for each project.

Finish
Allow project to dry (let the paint cure) at least 24 hours before applying varnish. Apply 1 coat of varnish. Let dry. Then apply second coat.
   On terracotta the gloss polyurethane waterbased varnish is the most effective and durable.

LEAVES

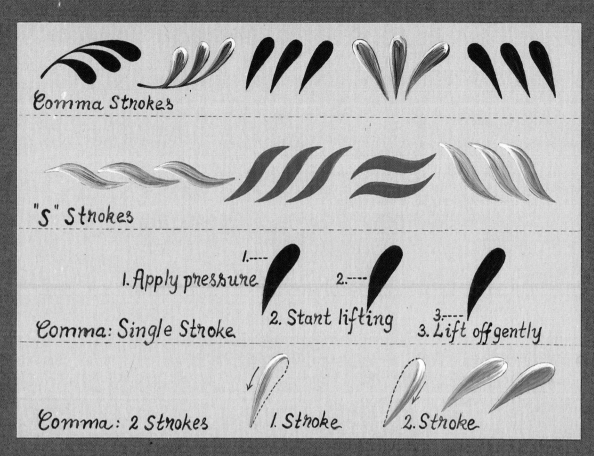

Comma Strokes

"S" Strokes

1. Apply pressure

2. Start lifting

3. Lift off gently

Comma: Single Stroke

Comma: 2 Strokes   1. Stroke   2. Stroke

Step by step leaves

Leaf borders and leaves: outlines on page 18

Leaf borders

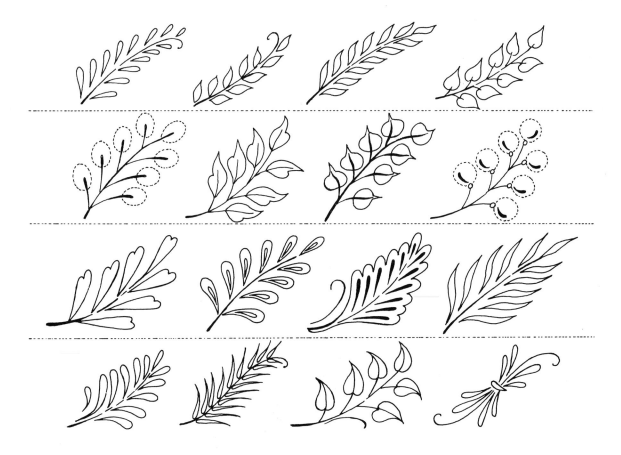

DAISIES

Daisy designs 1–4: oulines on page 22, instructions on page 24

5.

6.

7.

8.

Daisy designs 5–8: outlines on page 23, instructions on pages 24 and 25

1.

2.

Daisy design outlines

3.

4.

5.

6.

Daisy design outlines

7.

8.

DAISY DESIGNS—
INSTRUCTIONS
See page 20

DESIGN 1

Palette
Leaves: Medium Green + Cold White
Petals: Dark Yellow + Warm White
Flower centre: Yellow + White + Brown + Black
Curlicues: Brown

Painting guide
1. Leaves: Double load green + white; with #4 and #2 brush paint leaves and stems (add a touch of brown to green).
2. Petals: Yellow + white; double load #4 brush, paint all petals.
3. Flower centre: With #2 brush paint white and yellow; fine brown dots with #00 brush.
4. Curlicues: Brown, use #00 brush.

DESIGN 2

Palette
Leaves: Dark Green + Brown + Cold White
Petals: Dark Blue + Cold White
Flower centre: Yellow + Warm White + Brown + Black

Painting guide
1. Leaves: Double load #2 or #4 brush with green + white, paint leaves.
2. Petals: Double load blue + white, paint petals with #4 brush.
3. Flower centre: Using #2 brush paint white + yellow; fine dots with #00 brush.

DESIGN 3

Palette
Leaves: Mid Green + Cold White + Brown
Petals: Dark Pink + Warm White
Flower centre: Warm White + Brown
Spray: Warm White

Painting guide
1. Leaves: Use #2 brush, double load green + white.
2. Petals: Double load pink + white, use #2 brush, paint all petals.
3. Flower centre: White + brown, use #00 brush.
4. Spray: White, use #00 brush.

DESIGN 4

Palette
Leaves: Dark Green + Light Green + Cold White
Petals: Base coat Blue
  then paint over with Cold White
Flower centre: Yellow + Red + Brown + Black
Curlicues: Brown

Painting guide
1. Leaves: Add a touch of brown to green colour, then double load green + white, using #4 brush.
2. Petals: Base coat with blue, then paint petals with white only, use #4 or #6 brush.
3. Flower centre: Paint yellow first, then red with #2 brush. Brown + black dots with #00 brush.
4. Curlicues: Brown, use #00 brush.

See page 21

DESIGN 5

Palette
Leaves: Dark Green
Daisy base: Dark Blue
Petals: Cold White
Flower centre: Yellow + Gold
Curlicues: Brown

Painting guide
1. Leaves: Solid green, paint with #00 and #2 brush all leaves and stems.
2. Daisy base: Solid blue, use #2 brush.
3. Petals: White, use #2 brush.
4. Centre: Yellow + gold dots, use #00 brush.
5. Curlicues: Brown, use #00 brush.

DESIGN 6

Palette
Leaves: Medium Green + Cold White
Comma strokes: Dark Green
Petals: Mid Blue
Lines in petals: Dark Blue
Flower centre: Dark Blue + Cold White + Brown

Painting guide
1. Leaves: Double load green + white, use #2 or #4 brush.
2. Comma strokes: Solid green, use #00 brush.
3. Petals: Solid blue, paint with #4 brush.
4. Lines in petals: Dark blue, use #00 brush.
5. Flower centre: Dark blue and white dots, + touch of brown, use #00 brush.

DESIGN 7

Palette

Leaves: Green + Pale Green + Cold White
Petals: Mid Pink + Warm White
Flower centre: Yellow + White + Brown
Curlicues: Green + Brown

Painting guide

1. Leaves: Double load green + white, paint with #2 brush.
2. Petals: Double load pink + white, use #2 brush.
3. Flower centre: Yellow, white, brown + a touch of pink, use #00 brush.
4. Curlicues: Brown, use #00 brush.

DESIGN 8

Palette

Leaves: Medium Green + Dark Green
Petals: Pale Blue + Cold White
Flower centres: Cold White + Dark Blue + Brown
Stems, curlicues: Green + Brown

Painting guide

1. Leaves: Solid green, use #00 or #2 brush.
2. Petals: Double load blue + white, paint with #2 or #4 brush.
3. Flower centre: White with dark blue dots, use #00 brush.
4. Stems and curlicues: Green + Brown, use #00 brush.

SMALL DAISY DESIGNS— INSTRUCTIONS
See page 26

DESIGN 1

Palette

Leaves: Medium Green
Petals: Blue + Cold White
Flower centre: Yellow + Warm White + Brown + Gold

Painting guide

1. Leaves: Paint all leaves and stems solid green, use #00 brush.
2. Petals: Double load blue + white and paint all petals with #2 brush.
3. Flower centres: Yellow, white, brown and gold, use #00 brush.

DESIGN 2

Palette

Leaves: Dark Green
Petals: Cold White
Flower centre: Dark Blue
Dots: White + Gold

Painting guide

1. Leaves: Paint all leaves and stems with #2 or #00 brush, solid green.
2. Petals: White, use #2 brush.
3. Centre: Solid blue, use #2 brush.
4. Dots: White and gold, use #00 brush.

DESIGN 3

Palette

Leaves: Pale Green + Cold White
Petals: Pale Blue + Cold White
Flower centre: Warm White + Yellow + Brown + Gold
Curlicues: Gold + Brown

Painting guide

1. Leaves: Double load green + white, use #2 brush to paint leaves.
2. Petals: Use #4 brush for petals, double load blue + white.
3. Flower centre: White, yellow, brown and gold, use #00 brush.
4. Curlicues: Gold + brown, use #00 brush.

DESIGN 4

Palette

Leaves: Medium Green + Cold White
Petals: Blue + Cold White
Flower centre: Warm White + Yellow + Brown + Gold
Curlicues: Brown
Dot flowers: Cold White
Dots: Rich Gold

Painting guide

1. Leaves: Double load green + white, paint with #00 brush.
2. Petals: With #2 brush paint petals, double load blue + white.
3. Flower centre: White, yellow, brown and gold, use #00 brush.
4. Dot flower: White, use #00 brush.
5. Dots: Gold, use #00 brush.
6. Curlicues: Brown, use #00 brush.

Small daisy designs: instructions on page 25 and 28–29

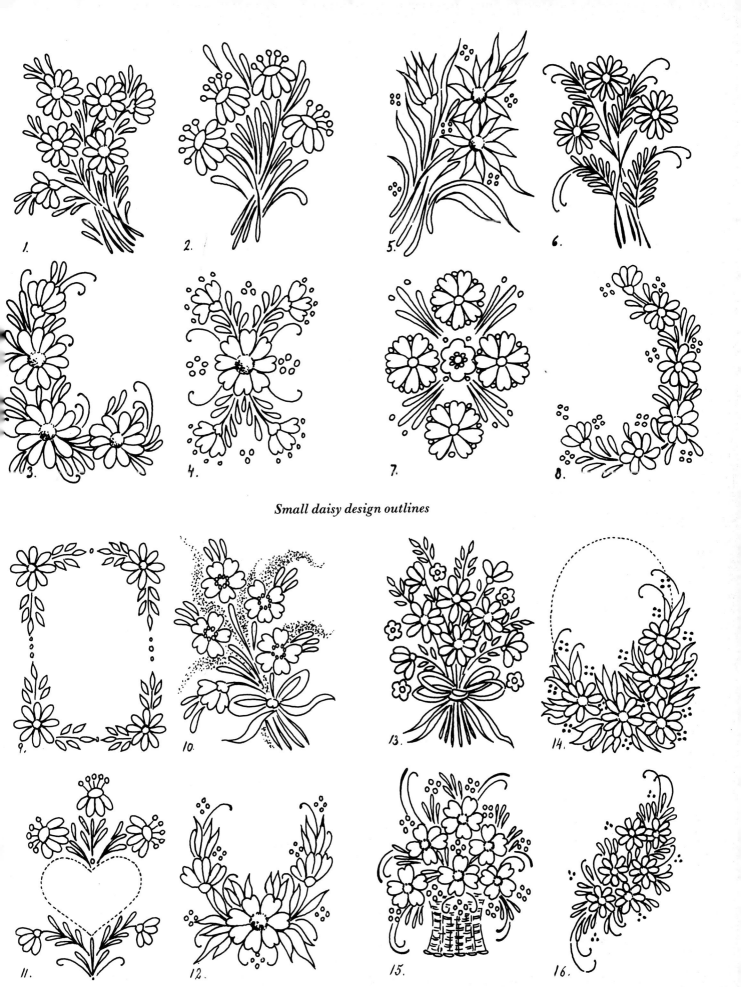

Small daisy design outlines

DESIGN 5

Palette

Leaves: Pale Green + Cold White
Petals: Antique Pink + Warm White
Flower centre: Warm White + Yellow
  + Brown
Dot flowers: Rich Gold

Painting guide

1. Leaves: Double load green + white, paint with #2 brush.
2. Petals: Use same brush, double load pink + white.
3. Flower centre: White, yellow and brown, use #00 brush.
4. Dots: Gold, use #00 brush.

DESIGN 6

Palette

Leaves: Medium Green
Flower base: Blue
Petals: Cold White
Flower centre: Yellow + Gold + Brown
Curlicues: Green + Brown

Painting guide

1. Leaves: Paint all leaves and stems solid green with #00 brush.
2. Daisies: Paint flower base in blue first, then paint white petals with #2 brush.
3. Flower centre: Yellow, gold + brown, use #00 brush.
4. Curlicues: Green + brown, use #00 brush.

DESIGN 7

Palette

Leaves: Pale Green + Cold White
Flower base: Dark Blue
Petals: White
Flower centre: Dark Blue
Small flower: Dark Blue
Dots: Gold

Painting guide

1. Leaves: Double load green + white, paint with #2 brush.
2. Flower base: Paint solid blue.
3. Petals: White, use #2 brush.
4. Flower centres: Solid blue, also centre flower, use #00 or #2 brush.
5. Dots: Gold and white, use #00 brush.

DESIGN 8

Palette

Leaves: Medium Green + Cold White
Petals: Yellow + Warm White
Flower centre: Orange + Warm White + Brown
Dot flowers: White

Painting guide

1. Leaves: Double load #00 brush with green + white, paint all leaves.
2. Petals: Yellow + white, double load #2 brush, paint all petals.
3. Flower centre: Orange, white + brown, use #00 brush.
4. Dots: White, use #00 brush.

DESIGN 9

Palette

Leaves: Medium Green + Cold White
Petals: Antique Pink + Warm White
Flower centre: Pink + Gold
Dots: Gold

Painting guide

1. Leaves: Use #00 brush, double load green + white.
2. Petals: Double load pink + white, paint with #2 brush.
3. Flower centre: Pink and gold, use #00 brush.
4. Dots: Gold, use #00 brush.

DESIGN 10

Palette

Leaves: Pale Green + Cold White
Petals: Pale Blue
Flower centre: Cold White + Dark Blue
Spray: White
Bow: Light Blue + Cold White + Gold

Painting guide

1. Leaves: Double load green + white, use #00 brush.
2. Petals: Pale blue, paint with #2 brush.
3. Flower centre: White with dark blue dots, use #00 brush.
4. Spray: White, use #00 brush.
5. Bow: Double load pale blue + white, use #00 brush, add a touch of gold.

DESIGN 11

Palette
Leaves: Dark Green
Petals: Dark Blue + Cold White
Flower centre: White
Dots: White
Heart: Orange

Painting guide
1. Leaves: Dark green, use #00 brush.
2. Petals: Double load blue + white, paint with #2 brush.
3. Flower centre: White, use #00 brush.
4. Dots: White, use #00 brush.
5. Heart: Solid orange, use #2 or #4 brush.

DESIGN 12

Palette
Leaves: Medium Green + Cold White
Petals: Orange + Warm White
Flower centre: Green + Cold White + Brown
Curlicues: Brown
Dot flowers: Blue

Painting guide
1. Leaves: Double load green + white, paint with #2 brush.
2. Petals: Double load orange + white, use #2 brush to paint petals.
3. Flower centre: White, green + brown, use #00 brush.
4. Curlicues: Brown, use #00 brush.
5. Dots: Solid blue, use #00 brush.

DESIGN 13

Palette
Leaves: Dark Green
Petals: Yellow + Warm White
Flower centre: Orange + Gold + Brown
Small flowers: Pale Blue
Centres: Yellow + Warm White
Bow: Pale Blue + Cold White

Painting guide
1. Leaves: Solid green, paint with #00 brush—all leaves and stems.
2. Petals: Double load yellow + white, use #2 brush.
3. Flower centre: Orange, gold + brown, use #00 brush.
4. Small flowers: Solid blue, white centres, use #00 brush.
5. Bow: Double load blue + white, paint with #00 brush.

DESIGN 14

Palette
Leaves: Medium Green + Cold White
Petals: Orange + Warm White
Centre: White + Gold + Brown
Curlicues: Brown
Dot flowers: White

Painting guide
1. Leaves: Double load #2 brush with green + white, paint all petals.
2. Petals: Use #2 brush, double load orange + white.
3. Centre: White, gold + brown, use #00 brush.
4. Curlicues: Brown, use #00 brush.
5. Dot flowers: White, use #00 brush.

DESIGN 15

Palette
Leaves: Dark Green
Petals: Antique Pink + Warm White
Centre: Dark Pink + Warm White + Brown
Curlicues: Brown + Gold
Dot flowers: Blue + Cold White
Basket: Yellow + Brown + Gold

Painting guide
1. Leaves: Solid green, paint with #00 brush.
2. Petals: Double load pink + white, use #2 brush.
3. Centre: Pink, white + brown, use #00 brush.
4. Curlicues: Brown + gold, use #00 brush.
5. Dots: Double load blue + white, use #00 brush.
6. Basket: Yellow, brown + gold, use #2 and #00 brush.

DESIGN 16

Palette
Leaves: Medium Green
Petals: Pale Blue + Cold White
Flower centre: Gold + Brown
Curlicues: Brown
Dots: Gold

Painting guide
1. Leaves: Solid green, use #00 brush.
2. Petals: Double load blue + white, paint with #00 brush.
3. Flower centre: Gold + brown, use #00 brush.
4. Curlicues: Brown, use #00 brush.
5. Dots: Gold, use #00 brush.

1.

2.

3.

4.

Daisy borders: instructions on page 32

5.

6.

7.

8.

1.

2.

3.

4.

Daisy border outlines

5.

6.

7.

8.

DAISY BORDERS—
INSTRUCTIONS
See page 30

DESIGN 1

Palette
Leaves: Pale Green + Cold White
Petals: Yellow + Warm White
Flower centre: Orange + Brown
Dots: White

Painting guide
1. Leaves: Double load green + white, paint leaves with #00 brush.
2. Petals: Use #2 brush, double load yellow + white, paint all petals.
3. Centres: Orange + brown, use #00 brush.
4. Dots: White, use #00 brush.

DESIGN 2

Palette
Leaves: Dark Green
Petals: Blue + Cold White
Flower centre: Yellow + Warm White + Brown
Curlicues: Gold
Dot flowers: Gold

Painting guide
1. Leaves: Paint solid green with #00 brush.
2. Petals: Double load blue + white and with #2 brush paint all petals.
3. Centres: Yellow + brown, use #00 brush.
4. Curlicues and dots: Gold, use #00 brush.

DESIGN 3

Palette
Leaves: Medium Green
Small flowers: White
Centre: Yellow + Gold
Petals: Antique Pink + Warm White
Flower centre: Yellow + Warm White + Brown

Painting guide
1. Leaves: Paint solid green with #00 brush.
2. Small flowers: White, use #00 brush.
3. Flower centre: Gold, use same brush.
4. Petals: Double load pink + white and with #2 brush paint all petals.
5. Centres: Yellow + brown + white, paint with #00 brush.

DESIGN 4

Palette
Leaves: Dark Green + Cold White
Petals: Dark Blue + Cold White
Dots: Gold and White

Painting guide
1. Leaves: Double load green + white and with #2 brush paint all leaves and stems.
2. Petals: Use #2 brush, double load blue + white.
3. Dots: Paint some gold, others white with #00 brush.

DESIGN 5

Palette
Leaves: Medium Green
Petals: Yellow + Warm White
Dots: Gold

Painting guide
1. Leaves: With #00 brush paint all leaves and stems solid green with #00 brush.
2. Petals: Double load yellow + warm white, paint petals with #2 brush.
3. Dots: Gold, use #00 brush.

DESIGN 6

Palette
Leaves: Dark Green
Petals: Cold White
Flower centre: Dark Blue
Dots: Gold + White
Curlicues: Gold

Painting guide
1. Leaves: Paint all leaves and stems with #2 brush in solid green.
2. Petals: White, use #4 brush.
3. Centres: Blue, use #2 brush.
4. Dots: Gold, use #00 brush.
5. Curlicues: Gold, use #00 brush.

DESIGN 7

Palette

Leaves: Medium Green
Petals: Blue + Cold White
Dots: Gold
Hearts: Orange or Red

Painting guide

1. Leaves: Paint leaves and commas solid green with #00 brush.
2. Petals: Double load blue + white and paint petals with #00 brush.
3. Dots: Gold, use #00 brush.
4. Hearts: Solid orange, use #00 brush.

DESIGN 8

Palette

Leaves: Medium Green + Cold White
Daisy base: Dark Blue
Petals: Cold White
Flower centre: Dark Blue + Gold
Dots: Gold

Painting guide

1. Leaves: Double load green + white, paint all leaves with #2 brush.
2. Daisies: Paint dark blue base first, using #2 brush. Then paint white petals.
3. Flower centre: Blue + gold, use #00 brush.
4. Dots: Gold, use #00 brush.

ROSES

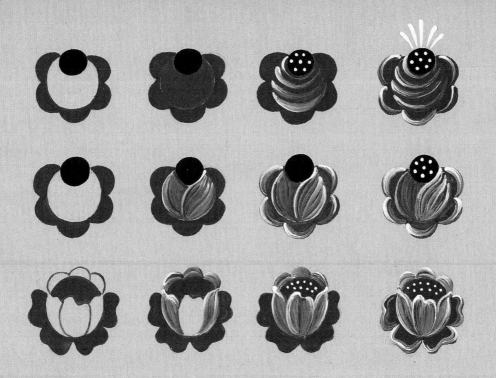

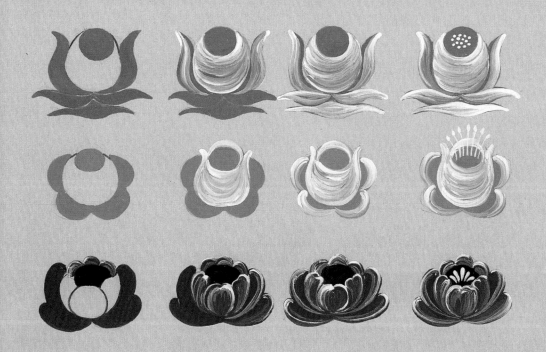

1.

2.

Rose design outlines: see page 40

3.

4.

5.

6.

Rose design outlines: see page 41

7.

8.

Rose designs 1–4: outlines on page 38, instructions on page 42

Rose designs 5–8: outlines on page 39, instructions on pages 42 and 46

ROSE DESIGNS—INSTRUCTIONS

See page 40

DESIGN 1

Palette
Leaves: Green + Cold White
Roses: Pale Pink + Warm White
Dots: Warm White
Bow: Pale Pink + Warm White

Painting guide
1. Leaves: Double load green + white, paint leaves and stems with #2 brush.
2. Roses: Use #2 brush.
3. Dots: With #00 brush paint white dots.
4. Bow: Double load #4 brush with pale pink and white

DESIGN 2

Palette
Leaves: Green + Cold White
Comma leaves: Green only
Roses: Antique Pink + Warm White
Bow: Antique Pink + Warm White
Dots: Warm White

Painting guide
1. Leaves: Double load green + white, paint larger leaves with #2 brush.
2. Comma leaves: Paint green only using #00 brush.
3. Roses: Paint centres of roses and outer petals pink with #2 brush first. Then double load pink + white, highlight bowl part of rose and petals.
4. Bow: Use #4 brush, double load pink + white.
5. Dots: Paint white with #00 brush.

DESIGN 3

Palette
Leaves: Green + Cold White
Roses: Rose Pink + Warm White
Bow: Rose Pink + Warm White
Spray: Cold White

Painting guide
1. Leaves: Use #2 brush, double load green + white.
2. Roses: Paint base for rose first with #2 or #4 brush. Then double load pink + white and paint the overstrokes.
3. Bow: Double load pink + white, paint with #4 brush.
4. Spray: With #00 brush paint white.

DESIGN 4

Palette
Leaves: Pale Green + Cold White
Roses: Pink + Warm White
Small flowers: Pink + Warm White
Flower centres: Pink + Brown
Bow: Pink + Warm White

Painting guide
1. Leaves: Double load #00 brush with green + white, paint all leaves and stems.
2. Roses: Paint centres first with #2 brush, solid pink first, then double load same brush with pink + white. Paint bowl part of roses and outer petals.
3. Small flowers: use #00 brush, double load pink + white, paint petals.
4. Flower centres: With #00 brush paint centres solid pink + add a touch of brown.
5. Bow: Double load pink + white, use #00 brush.

See page 41

DESIGN 5

Palette
Leaves: Dark Green + Cold White
Roses: Pink + Warm White
Buds: Light Pink + Dark Pink
Small flowers: Cold White
Flower centres: Yellow + Brown
Spray: Dark Green

Painting guide
1. Leaves: Large leaves to be painted with #4 brush, double load green + white. Use #2 brush for smaller leaves.
2. Roses: With #4 brush paint centre and outer petals of rose pink only. Then double load brush with pink + white, paint bowl part of rose and outer petals.
3. Buds: Use #2 brush, paint centres pink, then double load pink + white and paint rest of buds.
4. Small flowers: Paint white with #2 brush.
5. Flower centres: Yellow + brown, use #00 brush.
6. Spray: Paint green with #00 brush.

DESIGN 6

Palette
Leaves: Dark Green + Cold White
Roses: Dark Pink + Warm White
Rosebuds: Dark Pink + Warm White
Centres: Black + White
Curlicues: Rich Gold

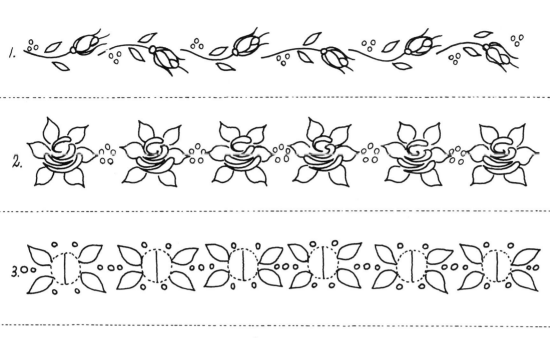

Rose border outlines: instructions on page 46

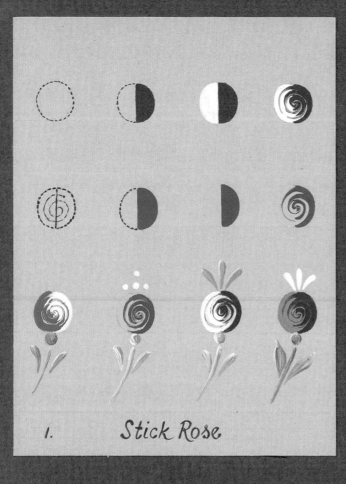

1. *Stick Rose*

2. *Éva's Rose*

3. *Rose Buds*

4. *Rose Buds*

Step by step rosebuds

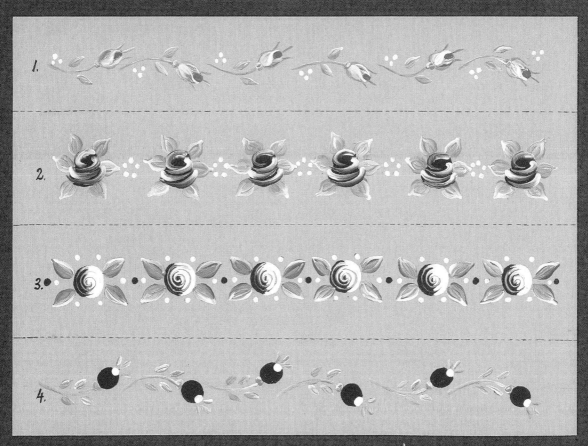

Rose borders: patterns on page 43, instructions on pages 46–47

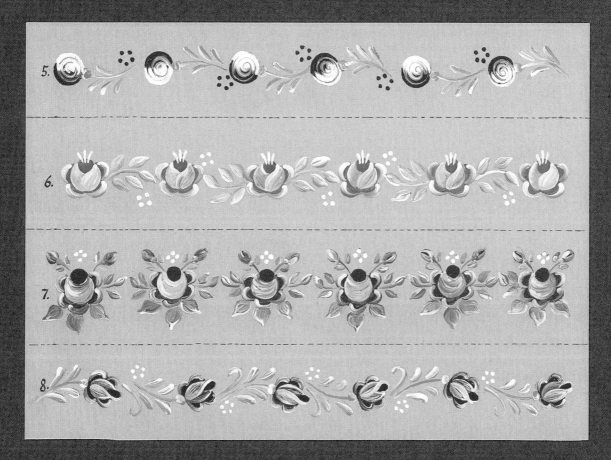

Painting guide
1. Leaves: Use #4 brush for larger leaves; some are solid green, others green double loaded with white. Paint smaller leaves with #00 brush.
2. Roses: Paint centre of rose black first, then double load pink + white and paint petals; use #4 brush.
3. Rose buds: With #2 brush paint centres black first, paint bowl part solid pink next, then double load pink + white and paint petals.
4. Centres: White, use #00 brush.
5. Curlicues: Rich gold, use #00 brush.

DESIGN 7

Palette
Leaves: Pale Green + Cold White
Roses: Rose Pink + Warm White
Small flowers: Pale Pink + Warm White
Dots: Green
Curlicues: Brown

Painting guide
1. Leaves: With #2 brush paint leaves, double load green + white.
2. Roses: Paint roses solid pink first, with #4 brush, then double load pink + white; use same brush, paint overstrokes and petals.
3. Centres: Brown lines + pink + white dots, use #00 brush.
4. Small flowers: Double load #2 brush with pink + white, paint all petals. Then add a touch of brown.
5. Dots: Green, use #00 brush.
6. Curlicues: Paint brown with #00 brush.

DESIGN 8

Palette
Leaves: Dark Green + Cold White
Roses: Orange Red + Warm White
Dots in centre: Warm White
Small flowers: Pale Orange + Warm White
Flower centres: Dark Orange
Dots and commas: Rich Gold

Painting guide
1. Leaves: Double load green + white, use #4 brush, paint all leaves.
2. Roses: Paint centres of roses and outer petals with #4 brush, orange first. Then double load orange + white and paint bowl part and strokes on the petals top and bottom.
3. Dots: White, use #00 brush.
4. Small flowers: With #2 brush paint petals; double load orange + white.
5. Flower centres: Dark orange, use #00 brush.
6. Dots and commas: Paint rich gold with #00 brush.

ROSE BORDERS— INSTRUCTIONS
See page 45

DESIGN 1

Palette
Leaves: Pale Green + Cold White
Rose Buds: Pink + Warm White

Painting guide
1. Leaves: Double load pale green + white, paint all leaves and stems with #00 brush.
2. Rose buds: Paint centres pink first with #00 brush, then double load pink + white and paint bowl part of bud with #2 brush.
3. Dots: White, use #00 brush.

DESIGN 2

Palette
Leaves: Green + Cold White
Roses: Antique Pink + Warm White
Dots: Warm White

Painting guide
1. Leaves: Double load green + white, use #2 brush, paint all leaves.
2. Roses: Paint base of rose first, solid pink with #2 brush, then double load pink + white and paint overstrokes.
3. Dots: White, paint with #00 brush.

DESIGN 3

Palette
Leaves: Green + Cold White
Roses: Pink + Warm White
Dots: Pink + Warm White

Painting guide
1. Leaves: Use #2 brush, double load green + white, paint all leaves.
2. Roses: Pink + white, use #2 brush and twirl with pencil.
3. Dots: Pink + white, use #00 brush.

DESIGN 4

Palette
Leaves: Pale Green + Cold White
Rose buds: Antique Pink
Dots: Warm White

Painting guide
1. Leaves: Paint with #00 brush, double load green + white.
2. Rose buds: Paint buds solid pink, use #00 brush.
3. Dots: White, use #00 brush.

DESIGN 5

Palette
Leaves: Pale Green + Cold White
Roses: Antique Pink + Warm White
Dots: Antique Pink

Painting guide
1. Leaves: Double load green + white and with #00 brush paint all leaves.
2. Roses: Pink + white, use #2 brush, twirl with pencil.
3. Dots: Pink, use #00 brush.

DESIGN 6

Palette
Leaves: Pale Green + Cold White
Roses: Pink + Warm White
Dots and commas: Warm White

Painting guide
1. Leaves: Use #2 brush; double load green + white, paint all leaves and stems.
2. Roses: Paint centre of roses and outer petals first in solid pink with #2 brush. Then double load pink + white and paint bowl part of rose and highlight petals.
3. Dots: White, use #00 brush.

DESIGN 7

Palette
Leaves: Green + Cold White
Roses: Rose Pink + Warm White
Buds: Rose Pink + Warm White
Dots: Warm White

Painting guide
1. Leaves: Double load green + white, paint larger leaves with #2 brush, smaller ones with #00 brush.
2. Roses: Paint centres and outer petals solid pink first, then double load pink + white and paint bowl part of roses and petals, also buds. Use #2 brush.
3. Dots: White, use #00 brush.

DESIGN 8

Palette
Leaves: Green + Cold White
Roses: Red + Warm White
Dots: Warm White

Painting guide
1. Leaves: Double load green + white, paint with #00 brush.
2. Roses: With #2 brush paint centres and outer petals solid pink. Then double load pink + white, paint bowl part and petals.
3. Dots: White, use #00 brush.

TULIPS

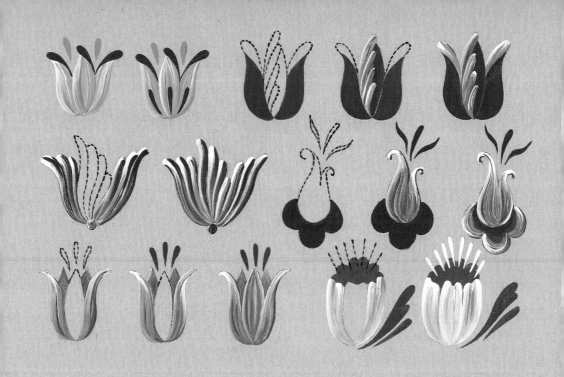

Step by step tulips

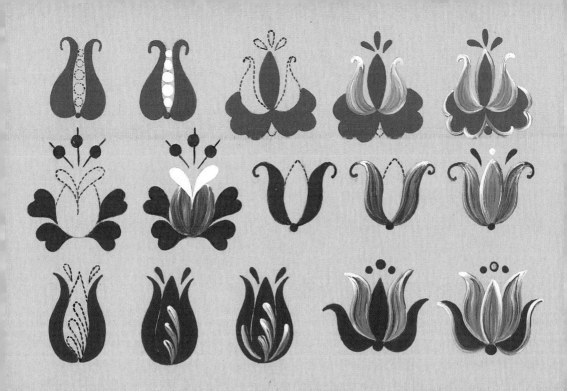

Step by step tulips

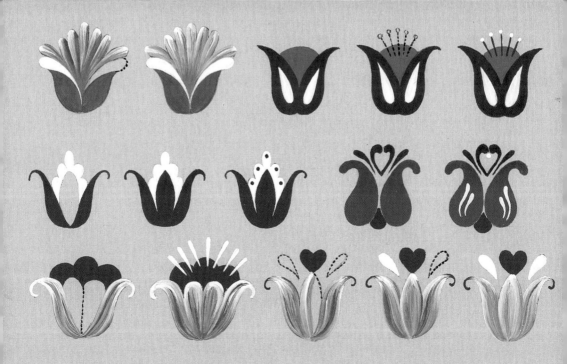

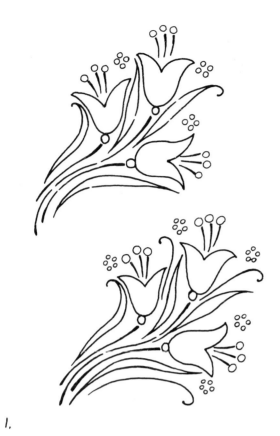

1.

2.

Tulip design outlines: see page 54

3.

4.

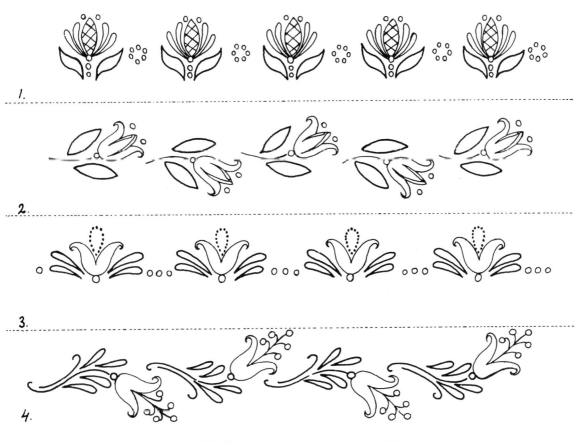

1.

2.

3.

4.

Tulip border outlines: see page 55

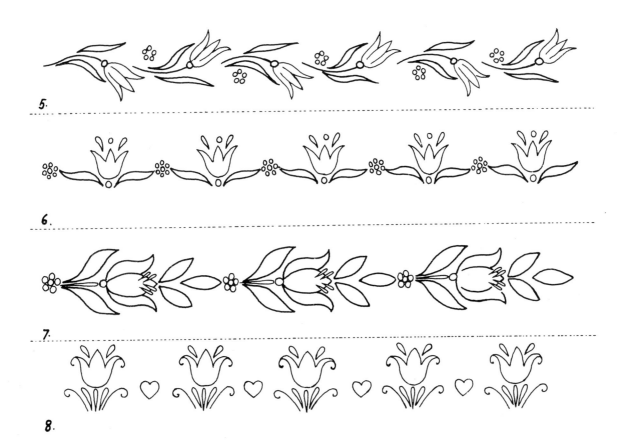

5.

6.

7.

8.

Tulip designs: patterns on page 52, instructions on page 56

1.

2.

3.

4.

Tulip borders: patterns on page 53, instructions on pages 56–57

5.

6.

7.

8.

TULIP DESIGNS—
INSTRUCTIONS

See page 54

DESIGN 1

Palette
Leaves: Green + White
Tulips: Antique Pink + White
Dots: White + Pink
Curlicues: Rich Gold

Painting guide A
1. Leaves: Double load green + white, using #2 brush.
2. Tulips: Double load pink + white, paint with #4 brush.
3. Dots: Pink + white, use #00 brush.

Painting guide B
1. Leaves: Solid green, use #2 brush.
2. Tulips: Paint solid pink with #2 brush.
3. Dots: Pink + white, use #00 brush.
4. Curlicues: Gold, use #00 brush.

DESIGN 2

Palette
Leaves: Dark Green + Gold
Tulips: Blue + White
Small flowers: Pale Blue + White
Flower centre: Gold + Brown

Painting guide
1. Leaves: Paint leaves solid green with #2 brush, highlight with gold.
2. Tulips: Double load blue + white; using #4 or #2 brush, paint outer petals first. Then paint centre solid blue; when dry, paint fine white lines with #00 brush.
3. Small flowers: Double load pale blue + white, paint with #2 brush.
4. Flower centre: Gold + brown, use #00 brush.

DESIGN 3

Palette
Leaves: Green + White
Tulips: Yellow Oxide + White
Small tulips: Orange

Painting guide
1. Leaves: Double load green + white, paint with #2 and #00 brush.

2. Tulips: Paint solid centre part of tulips first. Then double load yellow + white, use #2 or #4 brush.
3. Small tulips: Orange, use #00 brush.
4. Small commas: Gold, use #00 brush.

DESIGN 4

Palette
Leaves: Green + White
Mom: Orange + White
Flower centre: White + Brown + Orange
Spray: Rich Gold

Painting guide
1. Leaves: Double load #2 brush with green + white, paint all leaves and stems.
2. Mom: Paint solid orange centre part of flower first, then double load #4 or #2 brush with orange + white and paint all petals.
3. Flower centre: White dots, brown lines and orange dots, use #00 brush.
4. Spray: Gold, use #00 or #000 brush.

TULIP BORDERS—
INSTRUCTIONS

See page 55

DESIGN 1

Palette
Leaves: Green + White
Tulips: Antique Pink + White
Lines: White
Dots: Rich Gold + White

Painting guide
1. Leaves: Double load green + white, use #2 brush.
2. Tulips: Double load pink + white, paint outer petals first, then paint central petal solid pink, use #00 or #2 brush.
3. Lines: White, use #00 brush.
4. Dots: Gold + white, use #00 brush.

DESIGN 2

Palette
Leaves: Medium Green
Tulips: Rose Pink
Dots and lines: White

Painting guide
1. Leaves: With #2 brush paint leaves solid green, stem with #00 brush.
2. Tulips: Paint tulips solid pink with #2 brush.
3. Dots and lines: White, use #00 brush.

DESIGN 3

Palette

Leaves: Pale Green + White
Tulips: Rose Pink + White
Dots: Rich Gold + White

Painting guide
1. Leaves: Double load green + white, paint with #2 brush.
2. Tulips: Double load pink + white, paint outer petals with #2 brush. Then paint centre part pink.
3. Dots: Gold + white, use #00 brush.

DESIGN 4

Palette

Leaves: Dark Green
Tulips: Pink + White
Dots: White
Curlicues: Rich Gold

Painting guide
1. Leaves: Dark green, use #00 brush.
2. Tulips: Double load pink + white, use #2 brush, paint outer petals. Centre lines solid pink, use #00 brush.
3. Dots: White, use #00 brush.
4. Curlicues: Gold, paint with #00 brush.

DESIGN 5

Palette

Leaves: Green + White
Tulips: Blue + White
Dots: White

Painting guide
1. Leaves: Double load green + white, paint with #00 brush.
2. Tulips: Double load blue + white, use #00 brush.
3. Dots: White, use #00 brush.

DESIGN 6

Palette

Leaves: Dark Green
Tulips: Dark Blue
Dots: Rich Gold + White

Painting guide
1. Leaves: Solid green, paint with #00 brush.
2. Tulips: Paint solid blue, use #00 brush.
3. Dots: Gold, white + blue, use #00 brush.

DESIGN 7

Palette

Leaves: Pale Green + White
Tulips: Pale Blue + White
Dots and commas: White + Gold

Painting guide
1. Leaves: Double load green + white, use #2 or #00 brush.
2. Tulips: Double load blue + white, use #2 or #4 brush and paint all the tulips.
3. Dots and commas: Gold + white, use #00 brush.

DESIGN 8

Palette

Leaves: Green
Tulips: Mid Blue
Commas: White
Hearts: Rich Gold

Painting guide
1. Leaves: Solid green, paint with #00 brush, also curlicues.
2. Tulips: Paint solid blue with #00 brush.
3. Commas: White, use #00 brush.
4. Hearts: Gold, use #00 brush.

HEARTS

1.

A

B

C

D

E

2.

Heart design outlines: see page 62

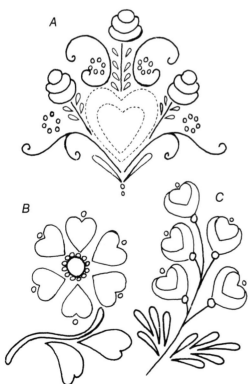

A

B

C

3.

4.

1.

2.

3.

4.

Heart border outlines: see page 63

5.

6.

7.

8.

Heart designs: patterns on page 60, instructions on pages 64–65

1.

2.

3.

4.

Heart borders: patterns on page 61, instructions on page 65–66

5.

6.

7.

8.

HEART DESIGNS—
INSTRUCTIONS

See page 62

DESIGN 1

Palette
Leaves: Dark Green + White
Mom flower: Pink + White
Heart: Pink + White + Gold
Dots and lines: Gold

Painting guide
1. Leaves: Paint solid green leaves first using #2 brush, then double load brush with green + white, paint rest of leaves.
2. Mom flower: Pink centre, then double load pink + white and paint petals using #2 brush. Fine lines are painted green with #00 brush.
3. Heart: Paint solid pink centre first, then double load pink + white, paint outer lines, use #00 brush.
4. Dots, lines: Gold, use #00 or #000 brush.

DESIGN 2

Palette A
Heart: Antique Pink + White
Commas: Dark Green
Curlicues: Gold

Painting guide
1. Heart: Paint solid pink first, use #2 or #4 brush. Then with #2 brush paint white outline.
2. Commas: Green, paint with #00 brush.
3. Curlicues: Gold, use #000 brush.

Palette B
Heart: Antique Pink + Gold
Dots and comma: Gold

Painting guide
1. Heart: Paint solid pink first, use #2 brush.
2. Dots, comma: Gold, use #00 brush.

Palette C
Heart: Rose Pink
Commas: Rose Pink + Rich Gold

Painting guide
1. Heart: Paint solid pink first with #2 brush.
2. Commas: Double load pink + gold, paint with #00 brush.

Palette D
Heart: Rose Pink + White
Leaves: Green + White
Rose and buds: Pink + White
Dots: Rich Gold

Painting guide
1. Heart: Paint solid pink first, use #2 brush. Then paint white scallops with #00 brush.
2. Leaves: Double load green + white, use #00 brush.
3. Rose and buds: Double load pink + white, paint with #00 brush.
4. Dots: Gold, use #00 brush.

Palette E
Heart: Dark Pink + Gold
Leaves: Dark Green
Comma and S stroke: Dark Green

Painting guide
1. Heart: Paint solid pink first, use #2 or #4 brush. Then paint gold outlines and commas in heart with #00 brush.
2. Leaves: Dark green, use #00 brush.
3. Comma and S stroke: Dark green, use #00 brush.

DESIGN 3

Palette A
Heart: Red
Roses: Red + White
Leaves: Dark Green
Curlicues: Dark Green
Dots: Rich Gold

Painting guide
1. Heart: Paint solid red, use #2 brush.
2. Roses: Paint solid red centre first, then double load red + white, use #00 brush.
3. Leaves: Dark green, use #00 brush.
4. Curlicues: Paint green with #000 brush.
5. Dots: Gold, use #00 brush.

Palette B
Hearts: Red
Centre: Gold + White
Leaves: Green + White

Painting guide
1. Hearts: Paint solid red, use #2 brush.
2. Centre: Paint gold first, then add white dots. Use #00 brush for dots.
3. Leaves: Double load green + white, paint with #2 brush.

Palette C
Hearts: Red + White
Leaves and stems: Dark Green
Dots: Rich Gold

Painting guide
1. Hearts: Paint solid red first, using #00 brush, then paint white.
2. Leaves and stems: Solid green, use #00 brush.
3. Dots: Gold, use #00 brush.

DESIGN 4

Palette
Hearts: Red + White + Gold
Tulips: Red + White
Blue flowers: Blue + White + Yellow
Leaves: Dark Green
Commas and dots: Rich Gold

Painting guide
1. Heart: Paint centre heart solid red, use #2 or #4 brush. Then paint white outline with #00 brush, fine lines with #00 brush.
2. Tulips: Paint hearts in tulip centres solid red. Then double load red + white and paint petals. Use #2 brush.
3. Blue flowers: Double load blue + white, paint petals with #00 brush. Then paint centres yellow + white; use same brush.
4. Leaves: Paint all leaves solid green, use #00 and #000 brush.
5. Commas: Gold, use #00 brush.
6. Dots: Gold, use #00 brush.

HEART BORDERS— INSTRUCTIONS
See page 63

DESIGN 1

Palette
Leaves: Dark Green
Hearts: Red
Dots: Gold + White

Painting guide
1. Leaves: Paint leaves, commas solid green with #00 brush.
2. Hearts: Solid red, use #2 brush.
3. Dots: Gold + white, use #00 brush.

DESIGN 2

Palette
Leaves: Medium Green
Hearts: Orange Red
Dots: Gold

Painting guide
1. Leaves: Solid green, use #00 brush.
2. Hearts: Paint solid red, with #2 brush.
3. Dots: Gold, use #00 brush.

DESIGN 3

Palette
Stems: Dark Green
Hearts: Rose Pink + White
Bow: Rich Gold

Painting guide
1. Stems: Solid green, use #00 brush.
2. Hearts: Paint solid pink, use #2 brush; for white centre part use #00 brush.
3. Bow: Gold, use #00 brush.

DESIGN 4

Palette
Leaves: Green
Hearts: Orange, Red
Dots: White + Gold

Painting guide
1. Leaves: Paint solid green with #00 brush.
2. Hearts: Solid red, paint with #2 brush.
3. Dots: White + gold, use #00 brush.

DESIGN 5

Palette
Leaves: Dark Green
Hearts: Dark Red
Dots: White + Rich Gold

Painting guide
1. Leaves: Solid green, use #00 brush.
2. Hearts: Paint solid red with #2 brush.
3. Dots: White + gold, use #00 brush.

DESIGN 6

Palette
Stems: Dark Green
Hearts: Red
Dots: White + Green
Bow: Rich Gold

Painting guide
1. Stems: Solid green, use #00 brush.
2. Hearts: paint solid red, use #00 brush.
3. Dots: White + green, use #00 brush.
4. Bow: Paint gold with #00 brush.

DESIGN 7

Palette
Leaves: Dark green
Hearts: Red
Dots: White

Painting guide
1. Leaves: Solid green, use #00 brush.
2. Hearts: Paint solid red with #00 brush.
3. Dots: White, use #00 brush.

DESIGN 8

Palette
Leaves: Dark Green
Hearts: Red
Curlicues: Dark Green
Dots: Rich Gold

Painting guide
1. Leaves: Solid green, use #00 brush.
2. Hearts: paint solid red with #2 brush.
3. Curlicues: Green, use #00 or #000 brush.
4. Dots: Gold, use #00 brush.

BIRDS

Bird designs 1–4: outlines on page 70, instructions on pages 72–73

Bird designs 5–8: outlines on page 71, instructions on pages 73–75

A

B

1.

A

B

2.

Bird design outlines

A

B

3.

A

B

4.

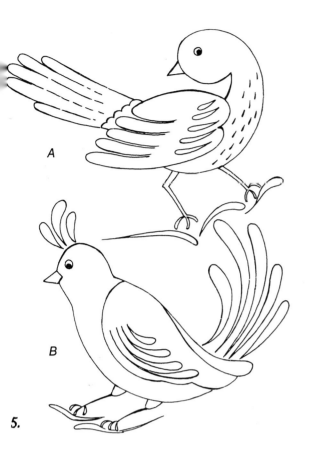

A

B

5.

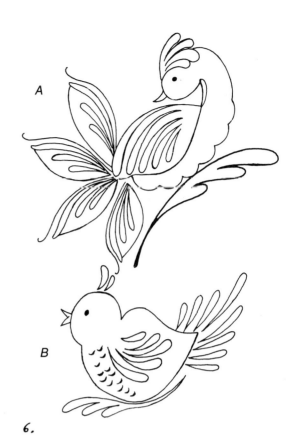

A

B

6.

Bird design outlines

A

B

C

D

7.

A

B

8.

BIRD DESIGNS— INSTRUCTIONS
See page 68

DESIGN 1

Palette A
Body, head and tail: Antique Green
Feathers: White + Gold
Beak: Pink
Eyes: Black + White
Cheek: Pink + White
Curlicues: Green + Gold

Painting guide
1. Body, head and tail: Solid colour, antique green, paint with #4 brush.
2. Feathers: White, use #2 brush.
3. Commas: Gold, paint with #00 brush.
4. Beak: Pink, paint with #00 or #000 brush.
5. Cheeks: Paint fine dots with #00 brush first in pink, then highlight with white.
6. Eyes: First paint small white circle with #00 brush, then add black dot and white dot to highlight eye. Paint eyelash with black, use #000 brush.
7. Curlicues: Dark green + gold, paint with #00 brush.

Palette B
Body: Rose Pink
Wing: Antique Green + Gold
Tail: Pink + White
Beak: Rich Gold
Eye: Black + White
Curlicues: Green + Gold

Painting guide
1. Body: Solid pink, paint with #2 brush.
2. Wing: Paint solid antique green first with #2 brush, then paint gold lines with #00 brush.
3. Tail: Highlight tail with white, use #00 brush.
4. Beak: Gold, use #000 brush.
5. Eyes: Black + white dot, use #000 brush.
6. Curlices: Green + gold, use #00 brush.

DESIGN 2

Palette A
Body: Turquoise
Wing: Blue + Gold
Tail: Blue + Turquoise
Beak: Pink
Cheek: Pink + White
Eye: Black + White
Curlicues: White + Green + Brown

Painting guide
1. Body: Paint body of bird solid turquoise, using #4 or #2 brush.
2. Wing: Solid blue, paint with #2 brush, then paint gold outlines with #00 brush.
3. Tail: Paint solid colours, blue + turquoise with #00 brush, then highlight with gold.
4. Beak: Solid pink, use #00 brush.
5. Cheek: Paint fine white dots with #000 brush, and add a touch of white.
6. Eye: Paint white dots first with #000 brush, then add a black dot.
7. Curlicues: White curlicue on bird, green + brown under bird, use #00 and #000 brush.

Palette B
Body: Blue
Wing: Turquoise + Gold + White
Tail: Blue + White
Beak: Rose Pink
Eye: Black + White
Commas on head: White
Curlicues: Green + Brown

Painting guide
1. Body: Solid blue, paint with #2 brush.
2. Wing: Solid colour, use #2 brush, then with #00 brush paint gold lines + white dots.
3. Tail: Double load blue + white.
4. Beak: Pink, use #00 brush.
5. Eye: White + black, use #000 brush.
6. Comma strokes on head: White, use #00 brush.
7. Curlicues: Green + brown, use #00 brush.

DESIGN 3

Palette A
Body: Blue + Gold
Tail: Yellow + White + Gold + Blue
Beak and legs: Red
Eye: White + Black
Leaves: Dark Green

Painting guide
1. Body: Paint solid blue with #4 brush. Then paint gold commas with #2 brush.
2. Tail: Double load yellow + white, paint with #2 brush; when dry, paint dots with blue + gold, double load #00 brush.
3. Beak, legs: Solid red, paint with #000 brush.
4. Eye: Paint white dot first, then black with #000 brush.
5. Leaves: Solid green, use #00 brush.

Palette B
Body: Yellow + White
Tail: Blue
Wing: Blue + Gold
Beak and feather: Red
Eye: White + Black
Leaves: Green

Painting guide
1. Body: Double load yellow + white, paint with #2 or #4 brush.
2. Tail: Solid blue, use #2 brush.
3. Wing: Double load blue + gold, paint with #00 brush.
4. Beak and feathers: Solid red, use #00 brush.
5. Eye: Paint white dot first, then black with #000 brush.
6. Leaves: Solid green, use #00 brush.

DESIGN 4

Palette A
Body: Rose Pink
Wing: Rose Pink + Gold
Tail: Pink + Gold
Beak: Gold
Eye: White + Black
Curlicues: Dark Green

Painting guide
1. Body: Solid pink, paint with #4 brush.
2. Wing: Solid pink, paint with #2 brush, then paint gold, use same brush.
3. Tail: Double load pink + gold, paint with #2 brush. Highlight other parts with gold, using #00 brush.
4. Beak: Gold, use #00 brush.
5. Eye: Paint white dot first, then black dot, use #000 brush.
6. Curlicues: Dark green, use #00 brush.

Palette B
Body: Rich Gold
Wing: Rose Pink + Rich Gold
Tail: Rose Pink + Warm White
Beak and legs: Rose Pink
Comb: Pink + White
Eye: White + Black
Curlicues: Dark Green

Painting guide
1. Body: Paint solid gold with #4 brush.
2. Wing: Double load pink and gold, paint with #2 brush.
3. Tail: Paint solid pink first, then white, use #00 brush.

4. Beak and legs: Solid pink, use #00 brush.
5. Comb: Paint pink first, then add white.
6. Eye: White + black, use #000 brush.
7. Curlicues: Dark green, use #00 brush.

See page 69

DESIGN 5

Palette A
Body: Red + White
Wing: Black + White + Gold
Tail: Black + White
Legs: Black
Beak: Gold
Eye: White + Black
Commas: Green + White

Painting guide
1. Body: Paint solid red with #4 brush.
2. Wing: Solid black, use #4 brush. Then paint commas gold, with #00 brush. Paint white with #00 brush.
3. Tail: Paint solid black first with #2 brush; then highlight with white lines, use #000 brush.
4. Legs: Solid black, use #00 brush.
5. Beak: Rich gold, use #00 brush.
6. Eye: Paint white dot first, then black dot; paint with #000 brush.
7. Commas: Double load green + white, use #00 brush.

Palette B
Body: Orange
Wing: Blue + White
Tail: Yellow + White
Head feathers: Yellow + White
Legs: Blue + Black
Eye: White + Black
Commas: Green + White

Painting guide
1. Body: Solid orange, paint with #4 brush.
2. Wing: Solid blue, use #4 brush, then paint white commas with #00 brush.
3. Tail: Double load yellow + white, use #4 brush to paint.
4. Head feathers: Double load yellow + white, paint with #2 brush.
5. Legs: Solid blue on top part, use #00 brush, and black at bottom part.
6. Eye: Paint white dot first, then black dot with #000 brush.
7. Commas: Double load green + white, use #00 brush.

DESIGN 6

Palette A
Body: Pale Blue
Wings: Dark Blue + Rich Gold
Tail: Pale Blue + Dark Blue
Beak: Orange
Head feathers: Dark Blue
Eye: Black
Comma: Medium Green

Painting guide
1. Body: Paint solid blue with #4 brush.
2. Wings: Paint dark blue, use same brush (#4), then paint gold commas with #00 brush.
3. Tail: Paint pale blue first, then dark blue, use #00 and #000 brush for fine lines.
4. Beak: Orange, use #00 brush.
5. Head feathers: Dark blue, use #00 brush.
6. Eye: Dark blue, paint with #000 brush.
7. Commas: Green, use #2 brush.

Palette B
Body: Pale Blue + Dark Blue
Wings: White
Tail: Blue + White
Beak: Orange
Eye: Dark Blue
Head feathers: Dark Blue + White
Commas: Green

Painting guide
1. Body: Paint solid with pale blue first, using #4 brush; then paint fine lines with dark blue, using #00 brush.
2. Wings: Solid white, paint with #00 brush.
3. Tail: Double load dark blue + white, paint with #00 brush.
4. Beak: Orange, use #00 or #000 brush.
5. Eye: Dark blue, use #000 brush.
6. Head feathers: Double load dark blue + white, use #00 brush.
7. Commas: Solid green, use #00 brush.

DESIGN 7

Palette A
Body: White
Wings: Pale Pink + Gold
Tail: Dark Pink + Gold
Beak and legs: Dark Pink
Eye: Black
Leaves: Green

Painting guide
1. Body: Paint solid white, use #00 brush.
2. Wing: Solid pink, use #00 brush, then with #000 brush add gold dots.
3. Tail: Paint dark pink first, then gold, use #00 brush.
4. Beak and legs: Dark pink, use #000 brush.
5. Eye: Black, use #000 brush.
6. Leaves: Green, use #00 brush.

Palette B
Body: Pale Pink + Gold + White
Wing: Dark Pink
Tail: White
Head: White
Beaks and legs: Dark Pink
Eye: Black
Leaves: Green

Painting guide
1. Body: Pale pink, use #2 brush, then double load dark pink + gold and paint lines near tail. Paint white scallops with #00 brush.
2. Wing: Solid pink, use #00 brush.
3. Tail: Paint white with #00 brush.
4. Head: White, use #00 brush.
5. Beak and legs: Dark pink, use #000 brush
6. Eye: Black, use #000 brush.
7. Leaves: Green, paint with #00 brush.

Palette C
Body: Pale Pink + Gold
Wing: White
Tail: Dark Pink + Gold
Beak and legs: Dark Pink
Eye: Black
Comma: Green

Painting guide
1. Body: Paint solid pink with #2 brush, then add gold dots with #000 brush.
2. Wings: White, use #00 brush to paint.
3. Tail: Dark pink, use #2 brush, then paint gold dots with #00 brush.
4. Beak and legs: Paint dark pink with #000 brush.
5. Eye: Black, use #000 brush.
6. Comma: Green, use #00 brush.

Palette D
Body: Dark Pink
Wings: Pale Pink + White
Tail: Pale Pink + White
Legs: Dark Pink
Beak: Rich Gold
Eye: Black + White
Comma: Green

Painting guide

1. Body: Paint dark pink with #2 brush.
2. Wing: Pale pink, then white lines, use #00 brush to paint.
3. Tail: Double load pale pink + white, paint with #00 brush.
4. Legs: Dark pink, use #000 brush.
5. Beak, commas on head: Gold, use #000 brush.
6. Eye: Black, with fine white dot, use #000 brush.
7. Comma: Green, use #00 brush.

DESIGN 8

Palette A
Body: Orange
Head: Pale Blue
Wing: Dark Blue + White + Yellow
Tail: Pale Blue + Dark Blue + Orange
Beak: Orange
Legs: Dark Blue
Eye: Dark Blue
Commas: Green + White

Painting guide

1. Body: Solid colour, use #2 brush.
2. Head: Pale blue, use #2 brush.
3. Wing: Paint yellow feathers first, then double load yellow + white, use #2 brush. Then paint solid blue + white line last.

4. Tail: Solid colours, use #00 brush for all three.
5. Beak: Orange, use #000 brush.
6. Legs: Dark blue, use #000 brush.
7. Eye: Dark blue, also paint feathers on head blue, use #00 brush.
8. Commas: Double load green + white, use #00 brush to paint.

Palette B
Body: Pale Blue + White
Wing: Dark Blue + Gold
Tail: Orange + White
Legs: Orange
Beak: Orange
Eye: Dark Blue
Commas: Green + White

Painting guide

1. Body: Paint body and head part pale blue with #4 brush. Then with #000 brush paint fine white lines.
2. Wing: Dark blue, using #2 brush, then with #00 brush paint fine gold lines.
3. Tail: Solid colour first, then highlight with white.
4. Legs, beak: Solid orange, use #000 brush.
5. Eye: Dark blue, use #000 brush
6. Commas: Double load green + white, paint with #00 brush.

WILDFLOWERS

Wildflower designs: instructions on page 80

1.

2.

Wildflower design outlines

3.

4.

WILDFLOWER DESIGNS— INSTRUCTIONS
See page 78

DESIGN 1

Palette

Leaves: Dark Green + White + Brown
Stems and curlicues: Dark Green
Violets: Mauve + Diox Purple + White
 + Yellow + Orange

Painting guide
1. Leaves: Paint leaves with #4 brush; double load white + green, add a touch of brown.
2. Stems and curlicues: Dark green, use #00 brush.
3. Violets: Paint violet first with mauve, use #4 brush, then double load brush with mauve + purple, paint over petals again.
4. Flower centre: Orange first, then paint teardrop strokes with #00 brush, double load yellow + white.

DESIGN 2

Palette

Leaves: Dark Green + Light Green + Brown
Flowers: Blue + White
Flower centre: Yellow + White + Brown
Bow: Pink + White

Painting guide
1. Leaves: Paint all leaves with suggested colours; use #00 or #000 brush.
2. Flowers: Paint petals first with blue, then double load blue + white, paint overpetals, use #2 brush.
3. Flower centres: Use #00 brush, double load yellow + white, add a touch of brown to highlight centres.
4. Bow: Double load pink + white, use #2 brush.

DESIGN 3

Palette

Leaves and flower base: Dark Green + Light Green
Flowers: Blue + White
Curlicues: Rich Gold

Painting guide
1. Leaves and flower base: Solid dark green, paint with #2 and #00 brush.
2. Flowers: Paint petals first with blue, then double load blue + white, paint over all the petals, using #4 or #2 brush.
3. Curlicues: Rich gold, use #00 brush.

DESIGN 4

Palette

Leaves: Dark Green + Light Green + White + Brown
Flowers: Light Blue + Dark Blue + Black + White
Flower centre: Yellow + White
Small flowers: White
Bow: Pale Blue + White

Painting guide
1. Leaves: Paint all leaves with #4 brush, double load green + white, add a touch of brown as well. Paint stems with #00 brush.
2. Flowers: Paint flowers first with light blue, use #4 brush, then double load blue + white, paint over petals, using #2 brush add black.
3. Flower centre: Yellow + white, use #00 or #000 brush.
4. Small flowers: White, use #00 brush.
5. Bow: Double load pale blue + white, use #2 or #00 brush to paint bow.

WILDFLOWER BORDERS— INSTRUCTIONS
See page 82

DESIGN 1

Palette

Leaves: Dark Green
Flowers: Blue + White
Flower centre: Yellow + White + Brown

Painting guide
1. Leaves: Paint green leaves with #00 brush.
2. Flowers: Double load blue + white, use #2 brush to paint flower petals.
3. Flower centre: Yellow + white, use #00 or #000 brush, add a touch of brown to highlight centre.

DESIGN 2

Palette

Leaves: Dark Green
Flowers: Blue + White
Flower centre: Yellow + White + Brown
Ribbon: Rich Gold

Painting guide
1. Leaves: Paint green leaves with #00 brush.
2. Flowers: Double load blue + white, use #2 brush to paint flower petals.

3. Flower centre: Yellow + white, use #00 or #000 brush, add a touch of brown to highlight centre.
4. Ribbon: Rich gold, paint with #00 brush.

DESIGN 3

Palette
Leaves: Dark Green + White
Flowers: Mauve + Purple + White
Flower centre: Orange + Yellow + White
Dots: Rich Gold

Painting guide
1. Leaves: Paint small commas and stems first, dark green only, use #00 brush. Then double load #2 brush with green + white.
2. Flowers: Paint all petals mauve first, then double load mauve + purple, also add a touch of white on the tip of your brush. Paint over all the petals. Highlight edges with white.
3. Flower centre: Orange, use #00 or #000 brush. Then double load yellow + white and paint teardrops in centre of flower with #000 brush.
4. Dots: Rich gold, use #00 brush.

DESIGN 4

Palette
Leaves: Dark Green
Flowers: Mauve + Purple + White
Small flowers: Pale Blue + White
Dots: Rich Gold

Painting guide
1. Leaves: Paint leaves and commas solid green; use #00 and #2 brush.
2. Flowers: Paint all petals mauve first, use #2 brush, then double load mauve + purple and a touch of white on the tip of your brush and repaint all petals.
3. Small flowers: Pale blue + white, use #00 brush.
4. Dots: Rich gold, use #00 brush.

DESIGN 5

Palette
Leaves: Dark Green + Light Green
Flowers: Blue + White
Curlicues: Rich Gold

Painting guide
1. Leaves: Paint all leaves and commas dark green first, using #00 brush, then with light green paint fine lines, using #000 brush.

2. Flowers: Paint all petals blue first, use #2 brush, then double load blue + white and paint over petals.
3. Curlicues: Rich gold, use #00 brush.

DESIGN 6

Palette
Leaves and stems: Dark Green
Flowers: White + Brown

Painting guide
1. Leaves: Paint leaves solid green with #00 and #000 brush.
2. Flowers: White, use #00 brush, add a touch of brown near flowers.

DESIGN 7

Palette
Leaves: Dark Green + White
Flowers: Pale Blue + White + Black
Flower centre: Yellow + White
Dots: Rich Gold

Painting guide
1. Leaves: Paint all leaves with #2 brush, double load green + white. Stems are solid green, paint with #00 brush.
2. Flowers: Paint all petals blue first, then double load blue + white, paint over all petals, use #2 brush. With #00 brush paint lines in centre of flower with black.
3. Flower centre: Yellow first, then double load yellow + white, use #00 brush. Add black dot last.
4. Dots: Rich gold, use #00 brush.

DESIGN 8

Palette
Leaves: Green
Flowers: Pale Blue + White
Flower centre: Yellow + White + Brown

Painting guide
1. Leaves: Paint leaves and stems with #00 brush.
2. Flowers: Double load pale blue + white, paint all petals with #00 brush.
3. Flower centres: Yellow + white, use #00 brush, add a touch of brown near centre.

1.

2.

3.

4.

Wildflower borders: instructions on pages 80–81

5.

6.

7.

8.

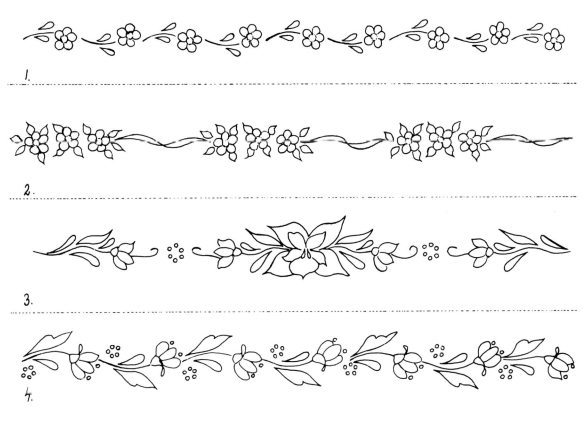

1.

2.

3.

4.

Wildflower border outlines

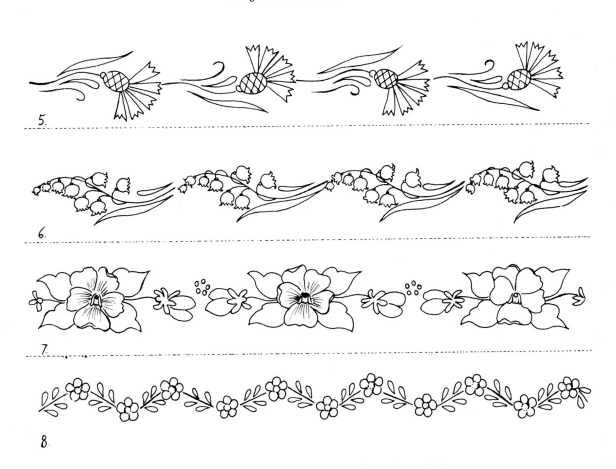

5.

6.

7.

8.

page 87

page 86

page 85

page 85

A larger floral alphabet appears on page 6

LETTERING

In folk art projects we often use wording such as 'Welcome', 'Bless This House', people's names and so forth. It is very important that your lettering blends in with the design. The lettering should be first of all readable and have a nice flow. For this reason I never use calligraphy, as it is hard to read and very stiff in style.

Besides using certain styles of lettering, you should try to write the words in your own handwriting, and stylise it as you paint them.

For painting use #00, #2, #4 brush depending on the widths of each letter, and instead of using just one colour, double load your brush. For example: green and white, burgundy and grey, red and gold, etc. However, when painting lettering with floral decorations, paint each letter first in the solid colour and let dry before painting the flowers on top.

'Oriental' alphabet

'Old English' alphabet

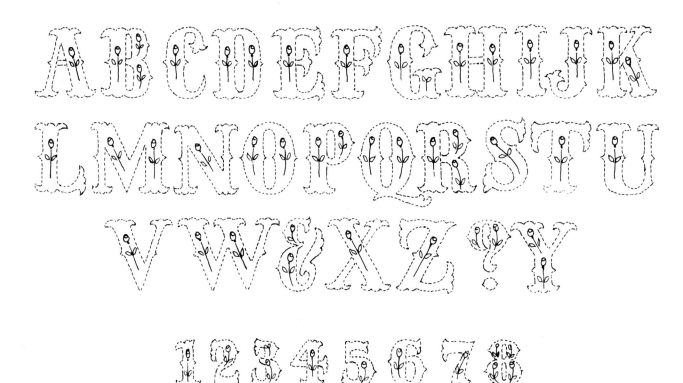

Rosebud alphabet

Italic alphabet

Index

Acrylic paints, 10
All-purpose sealer, 10, 11, 12, 14
Antiquing medium, 10
Apples, 8
Austria, 8

Baroque, 8
Base coating, 12
Basecoat colour, 10
Bauernmalerei, 7–8
Bavaria, 8
Berries, 8
Biedermeier, 8
Bird designs, 68–71
   instructions, 72–5

Carnations, 8
Comma strokes, 7, 10
Cows, 8
C-stroke, 11
Crackle medium, 10

Daisies, 20–7
Daisy borders, 30–1
Daisy designs, instructions, 24–5, 28–9, 32–3
Deer, 8
Ducks, 8

Eagles, 8

Farmer's painting, 8
Ferrule, 11
Fish, 8
Flow medium, 10

Grapes, 8

Heart borders, 62–3
   designs, 60–1
   instructions, 64–6

Leaves, 16–18
Lettering, 84–7
Lilies, 8
Liner brush, 11

Loading brushes, 11

Marbling, 12

Natural wood, 13
New tin, 13
New wood, 13

Old tin, 13
Old wood, 13

Pears, 8
Pencils, 12
Polyurethane varnish, 10, 11, 13, 14
Pomegranates, 8
Prepainted wood, 13

Renaissance, 8
Retarder, 10
Rococo, 8
Roosters, 8
Roses, 36–42
   borders, 44–5
   designs, instructions, 43, 46–7
Rubber, 12

Sandpaper, 12
Scrolls, 11
Sketch pad, 12
Sponging, 12
Staining, 13
S-stroke, 11
Switzerland, 8

Terracotta, 14
Tulip borders, 54–5
   designs, 50–3
   instructions, 56–7
Tracing paper, 12
Transfer paper, 12

Waterbased acrylic paints, 11
Wildflower borders, 82–3
   designs, 78–9
   instructions, 80–1